101
THINGS
GOD CAN'T
DO

Copyright © 1996 by James E. and Maisie C. Sparks

Published in Nashville, Tennessee, by Thomas Nelson, Inc.

Scripture quotations noted KJV are from The Holy Bible, KING JAMES VERSION.

Printed in the United States of America
10 9 8 - 03 02 01 00 99

101
THINGS
GOD CAN'T
DO

by Maisie Sparks

THOMAS NELSON PUBLISHERS
Nashville

ACKNOWLEDGMENTS

Without the loving support, encouragement and prayers of my friends and relatives, I could not have completed this work.

My special thanks to

My husband, James E. Sparks, who loves me and believes in me.

My pastor and his wife, Dr. and Mrs. Horace E. Smith, who said, "Do it!"

Suffragan Bishop Robert D. Young, Gaynel I. Young, and Marjorie C. Williams, who read the copy to ensure that I rightly divided the word of truth.

Everyone who has supported me in producing this second edition and who share my enthusiasm for telling the good news of what God can't do.

It's because God can't do these things that we can do

all things through Christ who gives us the power.

1. God can't lie.

That by two immutable things, in which it was impossible for God to lie, we might have a strong consolation, who have fled for refuge to lay hold upon the hope set before us.

Hebrews 6:18

2. God can't be given a problem He can't solve.

But Jesus beheld them, and said unto them, With men this is impossible; but with God all things are possible.

Matthew 19:26

3. God can't leave you.

And, behold, I am with thee, and will keep thee in all places whither thou goest, and will bring thee again into this land; for I will not leave thee, until I have done that which I have spoken to thee of.

Genesis 28:15

4. God can't forsake you.

...and be content with such things as ye have: for he hath said, I will never leave thee, nor forsake thee.

Hebrews 13:5

5. God can't despise a contrite heart.

The sacrifices of God are a broken spirit: a broken and a contrite heart, O God, thou wilt not despise.

Psalm 51:17

6. God can't allow His people to be ashamed.

And ye shall eat in plenty, and be satisfied, and praise the name of the Lord your God, that hath dealt wondrously with you: and my people shall never be ashamed.

Joel 2:26

7. God can't give His glory to anyone else.

I am the Lord: that is my name: and my glory will I not give to another, neither my praise to graven images.

Isaiah 42:8

8. God can't sleep.

Behold, he that keepeth Israel shall neither slumber nor sleep.

Psalm 121:4

9. God can't stop loving you.

...I have loved thee with an everlasting love: therefore with lovingkindness have I drawn thee.

Jeremiah 31:3

10. God can't go unnoticed.

The heavens declare the glory of God; and the firmament sheweth his handywork.

Psalm 19:1

11. God can't stand sin.

But your iniquities have separated between you and your God, and your sins have hid his face from you, that he will not hear.

Isaiah 59:2

12. God can't leave work unfinished.

Being confident of this very thing, that he which hath begun a good work in you will perform it until the day of Jesus Christ.

Philippians 1:6

13. God can't forget about you.

Can a woman forget her sucking child, that she should not have compassion on the son of her womb? yea, they may forget, yet will I not forget thee.

Isaiah 49:15

14. God can't be shut out of anywhere.

Whither shall I go from thy spirit? or whither shall I flee from thy presence? If I ascend up into heaven, thou art there: if I make my bed in hell, behold, thou art there. If I take the wings of the morning, and dwell in the uttermost parts of the sea; Even there shall thy hand lead me, and thy right hand shall hold me.

Psalm 139:7-10

15. God can't neglect His children.

If ye then, being evil, know how to give good gifts unto your children, how much more shall your Father which is in heaven give good things to them that ask him?

Matthew 7:11

16. God can't be put on a time schedule.

And he said unto them, It is not for you to know the times or the seasons, which the Father hath put in his own power.

Acts 1:7

17. God can't be given a job He can't handle.

Ah Lord God! behold, thou hast made the heaven and the earth by thy great power and stretched out arm, and there is nothing too hard for thee.

Jeremiah 32:17

18. God can't get weary.

Hast thou not known? hast thou not heard, that the everlasting God, the Lord, the Creator of the ends of the earth, fainteth not, neither is weary?

Isaiah 40:28

19. God can't be unknown to those who want to know Him.

And ye shall seek me, and find me, when ye shall search for me with all your heart.

Jeremiah 29:13

20. God can't lose anything.

And this is the Father's will which hath sent me, that of all which he hath given me I should lose nothing, but should raise it up again at the last day.
John 6:39

21. God can't make a loser.

Now thanks be unto God, which always causeth us to triumph in Christ.

II Corinthians 2:14

22. God can't be poor.

O Lord, how manifold are thy works! in wisdom hast thou made them all: the earth is full of thy riches.

Psalm 104:24

23. God can't give us a spirit of fear.

For God hath not given us the spirit of fear; but of power, and of love, and of a sound mind.

II Timothy 1:7

24. God can't be unloving.

He that loveth not knoweth not God; for God is love.

I John 4:8

25. God can't swear by anyone but himself, and He swore that He would bless you.

For when God made promise to Abraham, because he could swear by no greater, he sware by himself,

Saying, Surely blessing I will bless thee, and multiplying I will multiply thee.

Hebrews 6:13-14

26. God's love can't be measured.

For God so loved the world, that he gave his only begotten Son, that whosoever believeth in him should not perish, but have everlasting life.
John 3:16

27. God can't be equalled.

I, even I, am the Lord; and beside me there is no saviour.

Isaiah 43:11

28. God can't be silenced.

Our God shall come, and shall not keep silence: a fire shall devour before him, and it shall be very tempestuous round about him.

Psalm 50:3

29. God's word can't pass away.

Heaven and earth shall pass away, but my words shall not pass away.

Matthew 24:35

30. God can't be understood by human understanding.

O the depth of the riches both of the wisdom and knowledge of God! how unsearchable are his judgments, and his ways past finding out!

Romans 11:33

31. God's sheep can't be plucked from His hands.

And I give unto them eternal life; and they shall never perish, neither shall any man pluck them out of my hand.

John 10:28

32. God can't be imperfect.

Be ye therefore perfect, even as your Father which is in heaven is perfect.

Matthew 5:48

33. God can't think like you.

For my thoughts are not your thoughts, neither are your ways my ways, saith the Lord.

For as the heavens are higher than the earth, so are my ways higher than your ways, and my thoughts than your thoughts.

Isaiah 55:8-9

34. God can't be prejudiced.

Of a truth I perceive that God is no respecter of persons:

But in every nation he that feareth him, and worketh righteousness, is accepted with him.

Acts 10:34-35

35. God can't be beaten at giving.

Give, and it shall be given unto you; good measure, pressed down, and shaken together, and running over.

Luke 6:38

36. God can't be uncaring.

Like as a father pitieth his children, so the Lord pitieth them that fear him.

Psalm 103:13

37. God can't be seen by the natural eye.

For we walk by faith, not by sight.

II Corinthians 5:7

38. God can't be late.

Then said Martha unto Jesus, Lord, if thou hadst been here, my brother had not died.

Jesus saith unto her, Thy brother shall rise again.

John 11: 21, 23

39. God can't be second in your life.

Thou shalt have no other gods before me.

Exodus 20:3

40. God can't leave you comfortless.

*I will not leave you comfortless: I will come
to you.*

John 14:18

41. God can't forget those who serve Him.

For God is not unrighteous to forget your work and labour of love, which ye have shewed toward his name, in that ye have ministered to the saints, and do minister.

Hebrews 6:10

42. God can't be divided.

I and my Father are one.

John 10:30

43. God can't remember sins He's forgotten.

I, even I, am he that blotteth out thy transgressions for mine own sake, and will not remember thy sins.

Isaiah 43:25

44. God can't endure a proud look.

…him that hath an high look and a proud heart will not I suffer.

Psalm 101:5

45. God's mercy can't end.

O give thanks unto the Lord, for he is good:
for his mercy endureth for ever.

Psalm 107:1

46. God's name can't be taken in vain.

Thou shalt not take the name of the Lord thy God in vain; for the Lord will not hold him guiltless that taketh his name in vain.

Exodus 20:7

47. God can't allow anything to separate you from His love.

For I am persuaded, that neither death, nor life, nor angels, nor principalities, nor powers, nor things present, nor things to come, nor height, nor depth, nor any other creature, shall be able to separate us from the love of God, which is in Christ Jesus our Lord.

Romans 8:38-39

48. God's peace can't be understood.

And the peace of God, which passeth all understanding, shall keep your hearts and minds through Christ Jesus.

Philippians 4:7

49. God's word can't return to Him void, it will accomplish what He wills.

So shall my word be that goeth forth out of my mouth: it shall not return unto me void, but it shall accomplish that which I please, and it shall prosper in the thing whereto I sent it.

Isaiah 55:11

50. God can't be likened to anything.

Thou shalt not make unto thee any graven image, or any likeness of any thing that is in the heaven above, or that is in the earth beneath, or that is in the water under the earth.

Exodus 20:4

51. God can't change.

Jesus Christ the same yesterday, and to day, and for ever.

Hebrews 13:8

52. God's spirit can't always strive with man.

And the Lord said, My spirit shall not always strive with man, for that he also is flesh: yet his days shall be an hundred and twenty years.

Genesis 6:3

53. God can't deal with us according to our sin.

He hath not dealt with us after our sins; nor rewarded us according to our iniquities.

For as the heaven is high above the earth, so great is his mercy toward them that fear him.

Psalm 103:10-11

54. God can't be lost.

Jesus saith unto him, I am the way.

John 14:6

55. God can't make a mistake.

I know, O Lord, that thy judgments are right,
and that thou in faithfulness hast afflicted me.

Psalm 119:75

56. God can't let you down.

Now unto him that is able to keep you from falling, and to present you faultless before the presence of his glory with exceeding joy,

To the only wise God our Saviour, be glory and majesty, dominion and power, both now and ever. Amen.

Jude 1:24-25

57. God can't be left without a witness.

Yet I have left me seven thousand in Israel, all the knees which have not bowed unto Baal, and every mouth which hath not kissed him.

I Kings 19:18

58. God can't give imperfect gifts.

Every good gift and every perfect gift is from above, and cometh down from the Father of lights, with whom is no variableness, neither shadow of turning.

James 1:17

59. God's power can't be stopped.

And all the inhabitants of the earth are reputed as nothing: and he doeth according to his will in the army of heaven, and among the inhabitants of the earth: and none can stay his hand, or say unto him, What doest thou?

Daniel 4:35

60. God's word can't change.

For ever, O Lord, thy word is settled in heaven.
Psalm 119:89

61. God can't lose.

O sing unto the Lord a new song; for he hath done marvellous things: his right hand, and his holy arm, hath gotten him the victory.

Psalm 98:1

62. God's kingdom can't be destroyed.

Thy kingdom is an everlasting kingdom, and thy dominion endureth throughout all generations.

Psalm 145:13

63. God can't be unforgiving to those who ask for forgiveness.

If we confess our sins, he is faithful and just to forgive us our sins, and to cleanse us from all unrighteousness.

I John 1:9

64. God can't stop thinking about me.

How precious also are thy thoughts unto me, O God! how great is the sum of them!

If I should count them, they are more in number than the sand: when I awake, I am still with thee.

Psalm 139:17-18

65. God's plan for my life can't be bad.

For I know the thoughts that I think toward you, saith the Lord, thoughts of peace, and not of evil to give you an expected end.

Jeremiah 29:11

66. God can't break a promise.

My covenant will I not break, nor alter the thing that is gone out of my lips.

Psalm 89:34

67. God can't make junk.

And God saw every thing that he had made, and, behold, it was very good.

Genesis 1:31

68. God can't be impotent.

And I heard as it were the voice of a great multitude, and as the voice of many waters, and as the voice of mighty thunderings, saying, Alleluia: for the Lord God omnipotent reigneth.

Revelation 19:6

69. God can't be selfish.

He that spared not his own Son, but delivered him up for us all, how shall he not with him also freely give us all things?

Romans 8:32

70. God can't be dispassionate.

It is of the Lord's mercies that we are not consumed, because his compassions fail not.

Lamentations 3:22

71. God can't accept sacrifices when He asks for obedience.

And Samuel said, Hath the Lord as great delight in burnt offerings and sacrifices, as in obeying the voice of the Lord? Behold, to obey is better than sacrifice, and to hearken than the fat of rams.

I Samuel 15:22

72. God can't be the author of confusion.

For God is not the author of confusion, but of peace, as in all churches of the saints.

I Corinthians 14:33

73. God can't be unholy.

*And one cried unto another, and said,
Holy, holy, holy, is the Lord of hosts:
the whole earth is full of his glory.*

Isaiah 6:3

74. God's church can't be defeated.

And I say also unto thee, That thou art Peter, and upon this rock I will build my church; and the gates of hell shall not prevail against it.

Matthew 16:18

75. God can't be unfruitful.

I am the vine, ye are the branches: He that abideth in me, and I in him, the same bringeth forth much fruit: for without me ye can do nothing.

John 15:5

76. God can't be surprised.

But he knoweth the way that I take: when he hath tried me, I shall come forth as gold.

Job 23:10

77. God can't accept less than my whole heart.

And thou shalt love the Lord thy God with all thine heart, and with all thy soul, and with all thy might.

Deuteronomy 6:5

78. God can't be worshipped enough for who He is.

...and they rest not day and night, saying, Holy, holy, holy, Lord God Almighty, which was, and is, and is to come.

Revelation 4:8

79. God can't be surpassed.

Thus saith the Lord the King of Israel, and his redeemer the Lord of hosts; I am the first, and I am the last; and beside me there is no God.

Isaiah 44:6

80. God can't be overthrown.

Of the increase of his government and peace there shall be no end, upon the throne of David, and upon his kingdom, to order it, and to establish it with judgment and with justice from henceforth even for ever.

Isaiah 9:7

81. God can't be overruled.

Thy faithfulness is unto all generations: thou hast established the earth, and it abideth.

They continue this day according to thine ordinances: for all are thy servants.

Psalm 119: 90-91

82. God can't be matched.

For who in the heaven can be compared unto the Lord? who among the sons of the mighty can be likened unto the Lord?

Psalm 89:6

83. God can't be pleased without faith.

But without faith it is impossible to please him: for he that cometh to God must believe that he is, and that he is a rewarder of them that diligently seek him.

Hebrews 11:6

84. God can't be fooled.

For the word of God is quick, and powerful, and sharper than any twoedged sword, piercing even to the dividing asunder of soul and spirit, and of the joints and marrow, and is a discerner of the thoughts and intents of the heart.

Hebrews 4:12

85. God's righteousness can't end.

Thy righteousness is an everlasting righteousness, and thy law is the truth.

Psalm 119:142

86. God's burdens can't be heavy.

For my yoke is easy, and my burden is light.
Matthew 11:30

87. God can't let His people's prayers go unanswered.

If my people, which are called by my name, shall humble themselves, and pray, and seek my face, and turn from their wicked ways; then will I hear from heaven, and will forgive their sin, and will heal their land.

II Chronicles 7:14

88. God can't ask you to do something He can't do.

For it is God which worketh in you both to will and to do of his good pleasure.

Philippians 2:13

89. God can't be counselled.

For who hath known the mind of the Lord?
or who hath been his counsellor?

Romans 11:34

90. God can't be unfaithful.

They are new every morning: great is thy faithfulness.

Lamentations 3:23

91. God can't be figured out.

As thou knowest not what is the way of the spirit, nor how the bones do grow in the womb of her that is with child: even so thou knowest not the works of God who maketh all.

Ecclesiastes 11:5

92. God's salvation can't be earned.

For by grace are ye saved through faith; and that not of yourselves: it is the gift of God:

Not of works, lest any man should boast.
Ephesians 2:8-9

93. God can't be given less than all of me.

I beseech you therefore, brethren, by the mercies of God, that ye present your bodies a living sacrifice, holy, acceptable unto God, which is your reasonable service.

Romans 12:1

94. God can't be superseded.

And he is before all things, and by him all things consist.

Colossians 1:17

95. God can't be less than gracious.

The Lord is gracious, and full of compassion;
slow to anger, and of great mercy.

Psalm 145:8

96. God can't be impressed.

...and all our righteousnesses are as filthy rags; and we all do fade as a leaf; and our iniquities, like the wind, have taken us away.

Isaiah 64:6

97. God can't be insufficient.

Now unto him that is able to do exceeding abundantly above all that we ask or think, according to the power that worketh in us.

Ephesians 3:20

98. God can't be blamed if we don't make it to heaven.

How shall we escape, if we neglect so great salvation.

Hebrews 2:3

99. God can't take no for an answer.

Now the Lord had prepared a great fish to swallow up Jonah. And Jonah was in the belly of the fish three days and three nights.

Jonah 1:17

100. God can't fail.

Be strong and of a good courage, fear not,
nor be afraid of them: for the Lord thy
God, he it is that doth go with thee; he will
not fail thee, nor forsake thee.

Deuteronomy 31:6

101. God can't be praised enough.

Praise ye the Lord. Praise God in his sanctuary: praise him in the firmament of his power.

Praise him for his mighty acts: praise him according to his excellent greatness.

Praise him with the sound of the trumpet: praise him with the psaltery and harp.

Praise him with the timbrel and dance: praise him with stringed instruments and organs.

Praise him upon the loud cymbals: praise him upon the high sounding cymbals.

Let every thing that hath breath praise the Lord. Praise ye the Lord.

Psalm 150

Do you know something God can't do? Send it to us, along with the scriptural reference, and perhaps we'll include it in a future edition.

Send it to:
I Know Something God Can't Do
7115 W. North Avenue, Suite 335
Oak Park, IL 60302

Inquiries about speeches, seminars and book signings should be sent to Maisie Sparks, 101 Things God Can't Do, 7115 W. North Avenue, Suite 335, Oak Park, IL 60302.